A User's Guide to the Book of Common Prayer

Morning and Evening Prayer

Christopher L. Webber

morehouse

HARRISBURG • LONDON

Morehouse Publishing, P.O. Box 1321, Harrisburg, PA 17105
Morehouse Publishing, The Tower Building, 11 York Road, London SE1 7NX
Morehouse Publishing is an imprint of the Continuum International Publishing Group.

Library of Congress Cataloging-in-Publication Data

Webber, Christopher.
    A user's guide to the Book of common prayer : morning and evening prayer / Christopher L. Webber.
        p. cm.
    Includes bibliographical references (p. 47) and index.
    ISBN 0-8192-2197-X (pbk. : alk. paper)
    1. Episcopal Church. Daily morning prayer. 2. Episcopal Church. Daily evening prayer. 3. Morning prayer (Divine office)—Episcopal Church. 4. Evening prayer (Divine office)—Episcopal Church. I. Title.
BX5947.M67W42 2005
264'.03015—dc22

                                2005007377

Printed in the United States of America

01 02 03 04 05 06 07 08 09 10 11   6 5 4 3 2 1

Contents

NOTE: Complete commentary is provided only for Rite II Morning Prayer because it includes more material than does Rite I. In particular, it includes fourteen Canticles instead of seven. The discussion of Rite I in the introduction examines only the differences between the two rites. The Rite II commentary can be used for information about all of the material in Rite I.

Part I
Daily Morning Prayer

Introduction

Apart from the Holy Eucharist, Morning and Evening Prayer are the most familiar services of the Book of Common Prayer. But they are very different in character from the Holy Eucharist. The Eucharist is primarily an action in which we are involved, and, to a degree, an end in itself. Morning and Evening Prayer—also known as the Daily Offices, from the Latin word for "duty"—are more contemplative than active and are primarily a means for doing something else. They are intended to provide, first, a pattern for reading the Bible, and, second, a framework for our day.

In the 1979 Book of Common Prayer, the basic structure of Morning and Evening Prayer remains essentially unchanged from the pattern of the very first Prayer Book, compiled by Archbishop Thomas Cranmer in 1549. The 1979 Prayer Book provides two versions: one in traditional Elizabethan English (Rite I) and one in contemporary English (Rite II). No matter which version we use, no matter where we take part in the services—in a cathedral or parish church, at home, in an office, or on a commuter train—we are sanctifying time by framing each day with prayer. No matter the setting, the goal of the Daily Office remains the same: to provide opportunity for every Christian to offer each day to God.

A Pattern for Reading the Bible

In monastic communities, one of the reasons the monks prayed the Daily Offices was to read the Bible through in some systematic way. In the Middle Ages the growing number of saints' days interrupted the regular pattern of readings, and one of Archbishop Cranmer's objectives was to enable lay people to hear the whole Bible read.

Central to both Morning and Evening Prayer are the readings from the Bible. In Cranmer's plan there was to be one reading from the Old Testament and one from the New at each service. Most of the Old Testament and the Apocrypha would be read through each year, and the New Testament (except for the Book of Revelation) was to be read through three times each year. The psalms were divided into sixty segments so that by reading one at each service, morning and evening, the whole psalter could be read each month.

The 1979 Book of Common Prayer allows for the use of the thirty-day cycle of psalm readings but also provides a schedule that distributes the psalms over seven weeks through most of the year. Three Lessons, one each from the Old Testament, the Epistles, and the Gospels, are provided for each day with the suggestion that two be read in the morning and one in the evening. Following this pattern, most of the Old Testament would be read through in two years and most of the New Testament every year. Alternative plans include reading three Lessons at one service daily or two Lessons at both daily services. (See page 934 of the Book of Common Prayer for more information.)

The readings from the Bible are preceded by the psalms and separated and followed by Canticles. The Canticles provide opportunity to reflect on the readings while they are said or sung and to respond to the readings with praise. The readings and Canticles are followed by the Apostles' Creed, so that the readings lead to a statement of faith. The service then concludes with prayer. Morning and Evening Prayer are, then, biblical services: a way to read the Bible in a careful and systematic way as part of an offering of praise and prayer by the Christian community.

Just as the monastic offices were usually sung, so Morning and Evening Prayer have developed a rich heritage of music. Music adds to the beauty of the service, but there is also a very practical advantage to singing. Chanting the psalms and Canticles makes it easier to recite them in unison, and chanting the prayers makes it easier to hear the words, especially in a large church or cathedral. Evening Prayer, especially, is so often sung that it is commonly referred to as "Evensong." But while the Daily Offices may be elaborately sung, they may also be recited very simply by a few people in a small chapel or said privately by an individual with a Bible and a prayer book and ten or fifteen quiet minutes. Doing so frames our time in a Bible-centered pattern of prayer, shared in by countless Christians throughout the world.

A Framework for the Day

Time is God's most elusive gift: there is no way to hold it or change it. But we can measure it and, indeed, one of the psalms (104:20) suggests that God made the moon specifically to mark the seasons for us. If we can measure time, then we can also set aside a part of it to give back to God, just as we set aside parts of all our other gifts to offer them to the God who gives them to us. With time, as with money, we can find ways to set aside part as a way of showing that all of it belongs to God. The Sabbath was set aside as a way of making the whole week holy, and, in the same way, we set aside times of daily prayer to mark each day as God's. This marking and offering of time to God is an act of both stewardship and praise.

Christians inherited a pattern of daily prayer from the Jews, who set aside three times of prayer daily. But Christians found the psalm verse (119:164) that says, "Seven times a day do I praise you" and by the Middle Ages monks had developed a tradition of seven daily times of prayer:

Matins before dawn and Lauds at daybreak, combined into one service;
Prime, at the beginning of the work day;
Terce, Sext, and None at midmorning, noon, and midafternoon;
Vespers at sundown;
and Compline at bedtime.

Obviously, such a schedule could be kept only by monks and nuns, though lay people were encouraged to attend when they could.

In the first English Book of Common Prayer, Archbishop Cranmer set out to combine and revise the Daily Offices so that ordinary people could take part in them. The two new services of Morning Prayer and Evening Prayer would replace the sevenfold pattern and provide a way for everyone to praise God at the beginning and end of each day. These services, required for the clergy, became so popular that for centuries they pushed aside the Eucharist and even became the principal Sunday services, for both morning and evening. With the revisions of the 1979 Prayer Book restoring the Eucharist to its central place, however, Morning and Evening Prayer, in their turn, have often been pushed aside. As a remedy, the 1979 Prayer Book offers brief "Daily Devotions" for morning, noon, early evening, and close of day (BCP pages 136–140) and also restores the service of Compline to assist Christians who want a fuller structure of prayer for their daily lives.

How to Use Morning (and Evening) Prayer

For most Christians daily attendance at church morning and evening will be impractical, but the Daily Offices can be used at home (before breakfast or after dinner, for example) or in the office, or even while traveling. Longer and shorter versions can be used, as follows.

1 - Full Morning Prayer (Rite II)
Opening sentences (choose one or more), pages 75–78
Invitatory, page 80
Canticle (*Venite* or *Jubilate*, except *Christ our Passover* at Easter time), pages 82–83
Psalm (selections listed, pages 936 ff., or use the psalms for the day of the month, page 585 ff.)
First Lesson (selections, page 936 ff., or begin with Genesis and read a chapter a day)
Canticle (choose one), pages 85–95
Second Lesson (selections, page 936 ff. or begin with St. Matthew and read a chapter a day)
Third Lesson (optional)
The Apostles' Creed, page 96

The Prayers (Lord's Prayer and Suffrages, page 97, one collect, pages 98–100, one prayer from pages 100–101, other prayers optional)

Conclusion, page 102

2 - A Shorter Version of Morning Prayer (Rite II)

Opening sentences (chose one or more), pages 75–78

Invitatory, page 80

Canticle (*Venite* or *Jubilate*, except *Christ our Passover* at Easter time), pages 82–83

Psalm (selections listed, pages 936 ff., or use the psalms for the day of the month, page 585 ff.)

One Lesson (selections listed on page 936 ff., or begin with Genesis or St. Matthew and read a chapter a day)

The Apostles' Creed, page 96

The Prayers (page 97, one collect from pages 98–100, one prayer from pages 100–101, other prayers optional)

Conclusion, page 102

Morning Prayer, Rite I

The Rite I form of Morning Prayer differs from Rite II primarily in using traditional rather than contemporary language. The sequence of Opening Sentences, Confession, Invitatory, Psalm, Lessons and Canticles, Creed, and Prayers is exactly the same, although there are some differences in the Canticles and prayers provided. For a general discussion of Morning Prayer, then, the material on BCP pages 3–7 applies equally to both Rite I and Rite II. A few things, however, are different.

The same thirty-three verses of Scripture as Opening Sentences are provided for both rites. The first notable difference is in the Invitation to the General Confession (page 41 in the 1979 Prayer Book). This exhortation, essentially unchanged from 1552 to 1928, has been much shortened in the Rite I and II versions. In both, it lists the purposes for which we gather to render thanks to God, to praise God, to hear God's word, and to offer prayer. Oddly, the Rite II version omits the first of these purposes: "to render thanks for the great benefits that we have received." Since both versions include the General Thanksgiving, this difference cannot be explained.

The forms of Confession and Absolution in Rites I and II are different, but both are based on very ancient models. The Rite I Confession omits the words "and there is no health in us" and "miserable offenders" found in earlier prayer books. The first of these phrases especially is questionable theology, since it seems to imply that there is no goodness left in us as a result of our sins. Many Anglican theologians have maintained that the image of God remains present in every human being, though it is deformed or marred by sin. We are, one might say, "bent" but not "broken."

The *Venite* (see Glossary) has appeared in slightly different versions in different prayer books over the years. The first American prayer book dropped the last four and a half verses of Psalm 95 and added two verses from Psalm 96 in their place. The current Rite II version drops the verses from Psalm 96 and adds the half-verse of Psalm 95: "Oh, that today you would hearken to his voice!" The effect is to make the Rite I version center on God's holiness and worship and end with praise, while the Rite II version ends with a challenge to the worshiper. The traditional (pre-1928) version of the *Venite* (Psalm 95 in the language of the Great Bible, published in 1539) is also available on page 146 and, of course, the contemporary version is on page 724 with the other psalms.

The Canticles provided for Morning Prayer, Rite I, are all those provided in the 1928 Prayer Book for Morning Prayer as well as those provided in that book for Evening Prayer: the *Magnificat*, the *Nunc Dimittis*, and *Gloria in excelsis*. The *Gloria* was provided in 1928 only as an alternative to the *Gloria Patri* at the end of the psalms but is given here as a Canticle, perhaps on the theory that everything in the 1928 Prayer Book should be included somewhere in the 1979 Prayer Book. The Canticles added to the 1979 Prayer Book (numbers 8, 9, 10, 11, 14, 18, 19) have not been added to Rite I. Nevertheless any Rite II Canticle can be used with Rite I, and vice versa.

After the Creed and Lord's Prayer, the same two sets of versicles and responses are provided with, perhaps, one significant difference. The response to the last versicle in Set B in Rite II is, "And we shall never hope in vain." Rite I, less optimistically, says only, "Let me never be confounded." The first version is from the International Commission on English Texts, while the latter is a more accurate translation of the biblical text of Psalm 71:1.

Of the prayers, only two seem significantly dissimilar. The Collect for Grace is phrased very differently in the two services, though the same general line of thought seems to be followed. The General Thanksgiving in Rite II is modified for the sake of inclusive language by changing "to us and to all men" to "to all whom you have made."

The Daily Office

Daily Morning Prayer:
Rite Two

The Officiant begins the service with one or more of these sentences of Scripture, or with the versicle "Lord, open our lips" on page 80.

Advent

Watch, for you do not know when the master of the house will come, in the evening, or at midnight, or at cockcrow, or in the morning, lest he come suddenly and find you asleep.
   Mark 13:35, 36

In the wilderness prepare the way of the Lord, make straight in the desert a highway for our God.   *Isaiah 40:3*

The glory of the Lord shall be revealed, and all flesh shall see it together.   *Isaiah 40:5*

Christmas

Behold, I bring you good news of a great joy which will come to all the people; for to you is born this day in the city of David, a Savior, who is Christ the Lord.   *Luke 2:10, 11*

Behold, the dwelling of God is with mankind. He will dwell with them, and they shall be his people, and God himself will be with them, and be their God.   *Revelation 21:3*

Commentary

The title makes it clear that this is a service intended for daily use in the morning. The word *prayer* is used in the broadest sense as a synonym for *worship*. General directions on page 74 of the 1979 Prayer Book indicate that the service may be led by anyone, ordained or not, and that it is appropriate to assign individuals other than the leader to read the Lessons.

Opening Sentences

Since this is a service that centers on the reading of Scripture, the service appropriately begins with the reading of one or more sentences from the Bible. The service can also begin (as Cranmer's first version of the Prayer Book did) with the words "Lord, open our lips," found on page 80. When Cranmer added the opening sentences in 1552, they were all of a penitential nature and led into a General Confession. Beginning with the first American Prayer Book in 1789, a greater variety of sentences has been provided so that now there are sentences for every season of the Church Year and for "Occasions of Thanksgiving," as well as sentences to be used "At any Time." Since the Confession is now optional, these sentences can lead appropriately to the Invitatory. The only penitential sentences remaining are those designated for Lent.

Epiphany

Nations shall come to your light, and kings to the brightness of your rising.   *Isaiah 60:3*

I will give you as a light to the nations, that my salvation may reach to the end of the earth.   *Isaiah 49:6b*

From the rising of the sun to its setting my Name shall be great among the nations, and in every place incense shall be offered to my Name, and a pure offering; for my Name shall be great among the nations, says the Lord of hosts.   *Malachi 1:11*

Lent

If we say we have no sin, we deceive ourselves, and the truth is not in us, but if we confess our sins, God, who is faithful and just, will forgive our sins and cleanse us from all unrighteousness.   *1 John 1:8, 9*

Rend your hearts and not your garments. Return to the Lord your God, for he is gracious and merciful, slow to anger and abounding in steadfast love, and repents of evil.   *Joel 2:13*

I will arise and go to my father, and I will say to him, "Father, I have sinned against heaven and before you; I am no longer worthy to be called your son."   *Luke 15:18, 19*

To the Lord our God belong mercy and forgiveness, because we have rebelled against him and have not obeyed the voice of the Lord our God by following his laws which he set before us.   *Daniel 9:9, 10*

Jesus said, "If anyone would come after me, let him deny himself and take up his cross and follow me."   *Mark 8:34*

Holy Week

All we like sheep have gone astray; we have turned every one

The purpose of the opening sentences is to let a verse of the Bible provide the keynote of the service. The great number of sentences provided illustrates the perennial conflict between variety and sameness.

The Daily Offices are intended to sanctify our time. Is it more important to notice what is special about this particular day or to establish a pattern so unchanging that it can be said from memory? Obviously there are advantages either way. Perhaps the best solution is for individuals to settle on a sentence that changes only with the great seasons and major holy days if at all, while making use of the rich variety provided here for larger services and special occasions.

Routine may be what matters for individuals and small communities; too much variety can cause participants to wonder why a sentence was chosen, breaking their concentration. It may even be good to go straight to "Lord, open our lips," so that we are immediately involved in dialogue with God. Variety, on the other hand, can add to the special character of larger gatherings. Sentences can then be chosen to keynote the occasion.

Notice that the Easter Season sentences include one appropriate for Ascension Day and one appropriate for Pentecost.

to his own way; and the Lord has laid on him the iniquity of us all. *Isaiah 53:6*

Is it nothing to you, all you who pass by ? Look and see if there is any sorrow like my sorrow which was brought upon me, whom the Lord has afflicted. *Lamentations 1:12*

Easter Season, including Ascension Day and the Day of Pentecost

Alleluia! Christ is risen.
The Lord is risen indeed. Alleluia!

On this day the Lord has acted; we will rejoice and be glad in it. *Psalm 118:24*

Thanks be to God, who gives us the victory through our Lord Jesus Christ. *1 Corinthians 15:57*

If then you have been raised with Christ, seek the things that are above, where Christ is, seated at the right hand of God. *Colossians 3:1*

Christ has entered, not into a sanctuary made with hands, a copy of the true one, but into heaven itself, now to appear in the presence of God on our behalf. *Hebrews 9:24*

You shall receive power when the Holy Spirit has come upon you; and you shall be my witnesses in Jerusalem, and in all Judea, and Samaria, and to the ends of the earth. *Acts 1:8*

Trinity Sunday

Holy, holy, holy is the Lord God Almighty, who was, and is, and is to come! *Revelation 4:8*

All Saints and other Major Saints' Days

We give thanks to the Father, who has made us worthy to share in the inheritance of the saints in light. *Colossians 1:12*

You are no longer strangers and sojourners, but fellow citizens with the saints and members of the household of God.   *Ephesians 2:19*

Their sound has gone out into all lands, and their message to the ends of the world.   *Psalm 19:4*

Occasions of Thanksgiving

Give thanks to the Lord, and call upon his Name; make known his deeds among the peoples.   *Psalm 105:1*

At any Time

Grace to you and peace from God our Father and the Lord Jesus Christ.   *Philippians 1:2*

I was glad when they said to me, "Let us go to the house of the Lord." *Psalm 122:1*

Let the words of my mouth and the meditation of my heart be acceptable in your sight, O Lord, my strength and my redeemer. *Psalm 19:14*

Send out your light and your truth, that they may lead me, and bring me to your holy hill and to your dwelling.   *Psalm 43:3*

The Lord is in his holy temple; let all the earth keep silence before him.   *Habakkuk 2:20*

The hour is coming, and now is, when the true worshipers will worship the Father in spirit and truth, for such the Father seeks to worship him.   *John 4:23*

Thus says the high and lofty One who inhabits eternity, whose name is Holy, "I dwell in the high and holy place and also with the one who has a contrite and humble spirit, to revive the spirit of the humble and to revive the heart of the contrite."   *Isaiah 57:15*

The following Confession of Sin may then be said; or the Office may continue at once with "Lord, open our lips."

Confession of Sin

The Officiant says to the people

Dearly beloved, we have come together in the presence of Almighty God our heavenly Father, to set forth his praise, to hear his holy Word, and to ask, for ourselves and on behalf of others, those things that are necessary for our life and our salvation. And so that we may prepare ourselves in heart and mind to worship him, let us kneel in silence, and with penitent and obedient hearts confess our sins, that we may obtain forgiveness by his infinite goodness and mercy.

or this

Let us confess our sins against God and our neighbor.

Silence may be kept.

Officiant and People together, all kneeling

Most merciful God,
we confess that we have sinned against you
in thought, word, and deed,
by what we have done,
and by what we have left undone.
We have not loved you with our whole heart;
we have not loved our neighbors as ourselves.
We are truly sorry and we humbly repent.
For the sake of your Son Jesus Christ,
have mercy on us and forgive us;
that we may delight in your will,
and walk in your ways,
to the glory of your Name. Amen.

Confession of Sin

The Confession of Sin has three sections: a bidding or invitation, the confession itself, and the absolution. The bidding (which might appropriately be preceded at any time by one of the Lenten opening sentences) has both a long and a short alternative form. The longer bidding sets out the purpose of the whole service: to praise God, to hear God's Word, and to ask for ourselves and for others. The confession is then provided as a way to prepare ourselves to take part in this service.

Here and throughout the service, times of silence are suggested for individual reflection. The silence before the confession allows opportunity to recall our failures so that we can ask God's forgiveness for them.

The confession lists briefly the ways we fall short of our calling: by our thoughts, words, and actions, both done and left undone. In a busy world, we are all aware of the items remaining on our "to do" lists, but we ought to think as well of the actions that never get on our lists at all. How much of what we are aware of having left undone doesn't really need to be done, and how many other good things might we have done for God and others if we had loved God more?

Sorrow is expressed for our failures, since it is our sorrow and repentance that opens the way to God's forgiveness, which is always freely available to those who seek it. The confession ends by asking that forgiveness may lead us to let God direct our lives more fully and that we may delight in that guidance.

The Priest alone stands and says

Almighty God have mercy on you, forgive you all your sins through our Lord Jesus Christ, strengthen you in all goodness, and by the power of the Holy Spirit keep you in eternal life. *Amen.*

A deacon or lay person using the preceding form remains kneeling, and substitutes "us" for "you" and "our" for "your".

The Invitatory and Psalter

All stand

Officiant   Lord, open our lips.
People   And our mouth shall proclaim your praise.

Officiant and People

Glory to the Father, and to the Son, and to the Holy Spirit: as it was in the beginning, is now, and will be for ever. Amen.

Except in Lent, add   Alleluia.

Then follows one of the Invitatory Psalms, Venite or Jubilate.

One of the following Antiphons may be sung or said with the Invitatory Psalm

In Advent

Our King and Savior now draws near: Come let us adore him.

On the Twelve Days of Christmas

Alleluia. To us a child is born: Come let us adore him. Alleluia.

The absolution flows from the fact that it is God's nature to have mercy. This prayer of absolution moves on from pronouncing forgiveness to asking God to provide the strength to live a new life and to continue in the risen, eternal life given us in baptism but constantly in need of renewal. Forgiveness is not simply a way to deal with the past; it also to enables us to move into the future to which God calls us.

Notice that the absolution should be modified into a declaration of forgiveness when no bishop or priest is present by changing "you" and "your" to "us" and "our."

The Invitatory and Psalter

The Invitatory in the monastic office consisted of a set psalm and antiphon. Here the term is broadened to include the whole section from the opening sentences and confession to the psalms and readings. This may also be the opening movement of the service. Either way, it invites us to join in praise of God.

"Lord, open our lips" was the beginning of the monastic office and may still be used to open the service today. That verse and response are followed by two brief but powerful formulas that occur frequently in the Prayer Book: the *Gloria* and the *Alleluia*.

The *Gloria* (or *Gloria Patri*) is a one-sentence summary of Christian worship that can be traced to the fourth century and may have been suggested originally by the baptismal formula: "In the Name of the Father and of the Son and of the Holy Spirit." It has traditionally been used at the end of each psalm or at the end of all the psalms, and in other places as well.

From the Epiphany through the Baptism of Christ, and on the Feasts of the Transfiguration and Holy Cross

The Lord has shown forth his glory: Come let us adore him.

In Lent

The Lord is full of compassion and mercy: Come let us adore him.

From Easter Day until the Ascension

Alleluia. The Lord is risen indeed: Come let us adore him. Alleluia.

From Ascension Day until the Day of Pentecost

Alleluia. Christ the Lord has ascended into heaven: Come let us adore him. Alleluia.

On the Day of Pentecost

Alleluia. The Spirit of the Lord renews the face of the earth: Come let us adore him. Alleluia.

On Trinity Sunday

Father, Son, and Holy Spirit, one God: Come let us adore him.

On other Sundays and Weekdays

The earth is the Lord's for he made it: Come let us adore him.

or this

Worship the Lord in the beauty of holiness: Come let us adore him.

or this

The mercy of the Lord is everlasting: Come let us adore him.

The word *Alleluia* is a Christianized version of the Hebrew word *Hallelujah* (still used, of course, by Christians also and used in the 1979 Prayer Book version of the psalms), meaning "praise God." This word is traditionally never used in Lent and as a result it comes with special force when its use is restored at Easter.

Antiphons are verses of Scripture used as a refrain with psalms or Canticles. The seasonal and general antiphons can be used at the beginning and end of the fixed psalm or Canticle. The antiphon can provide a simple congregational response, which is especially useful if there is an elaborate musical setting.

Antiphons were originally Scripture verses sung antiphonally (back and forth) between two voices or choirs. They have come to be verses that emphasize the theme of the season and put the following psalm or Canticle within that frame of reference.

Antiphons may be used or not at the discretion of the one conducting the service. They may be used both at the beginning and end of the Canticle or only at the beginning. There are antiphons provided both for the various seasons, for special occasions of the Christian year, and for ordinary Sundays and weekdays.

The Alleluias in the following Antiphons are used only in Easter Season.

On Feasts of the Incarnation

[Alleluia.] The Word was made flesh and dwelt among us:
Come let us adore him. [Alleluia.]

On All Saints and other Major Saints' Days

[Alleluia.] The Lord is glorious in his saints: Come let us adore him.
[Alleluia.]

Venite *Psalm 95:1–7*

Come, let us sing to the Lord; *
   let us shout for joy to the Rock of our salvation.
Let us come before his presence with thanksgiving *
   and raise a loud shout to him with psalms.

For the Lord is a great God, *
   and a great King above all gods.
In his hand are the caverns of the earth, *
   and the heights of the hills are his also.
The sea is his, for he made it, *
   and his hands have molded the dry land.

Come, let us bow down, and bend the knee, *
   and kneel before the Lord our Maker.
For he is our God,
and we are the people of his pasture and the sheep of his hand. *
   Oh, that today you would hearken to his voice!

or Psalm 95, page 724.

Jubilate *Psalm 100*

Be joyful in the Lord, all you lands; *
   serve the Lord with gladness
   and come before his presence with a song.

A choice of three Invitatory Canticles is provided, though the third choice is ordinarily used only in Easter Season. The Prayer Book says that metrical versions (arranged for singing to hymn tunes) of the Invitatory Psalms and the Canticles may be used; a collection of metrical Canticles and psalms is available from Church Publishing. This might be especially helpful in small congregations with limited musical resources.

Venite

The *Venite* is a shortened version of Psalm 95, which seems to have been written for use in worship at the temple in Jerusalem. For at least 2,500 years, it has summoned God's people to worship. The earliest versions of the Daily Office include this psalm for the first office of the day. While the *Venite* does speak of the "God of our salvation," the emphasis is not on salvation but on God revealed in nature. God is known to us first as Creator, and it is the wonder of creation that we are made aware of with each returning day. It is the order and beauty and rhythmic pattern of nature that provide the first motivation for the regularity of the daily offering of prayer. Many believe that no better invitation to praise and worship than the *Venite* has ever been written. The whole of Psalm 95, with its warning against "hardening your hearts," may be used at any time and should be used on Fridays in Lent.

Know this: The Lord himself is God; *
  he himself has made us, and we are his;
  we are his people and the sheep of his pasture.

Enter his gates with thanksgiving;
go into his courts with praise; *
  give thanks to him and call upon his Name.

For the Lord is good;
his mercy is everlasting; *
  and his faithfulness endures from age to age.

*In Easter Week, in place of an Invitatory Psalm, the following is
sung or said. It may also be used daily until the Day of Pentecost.*

Christ our Passover   *Pascha nostrum*

1 Corinthians 5:7–8; Romans 6:9–11; 1 Corinthians 15:20–22

Alleluia.
Christ our Passover has been sacrificed for us; *
  therefore let us keep the feast,
Not with the old leaven, the leaven of malice and evil, *
  but with the unleavened bread of sincerity and truth. Alleluia.

Christ being raised from the dead will never die again; *
  death no longer has dominion over him.
The death that he died, he died to sin, once for all; *
  but the life he lives, he lives to God.
So also consider yourselves dead to sin, *
  and alive to God in Jesus Christ our Lord. Alleluia.

Christ has been raised from the dead, *
  the first fruits of those who have fallen asleep.
For since by a man came death, *
  by a man has come also the resurrection of the dead.
For as in Adam all die, *
  so also in Christ shall all be made alive. Alleluia.

Jubilate

As the *Venite* was a fixed part of Matins, so the *Jubilate* (Psalm 100) was part of Lauds and Prime. Both Canticles speak of us as God's "people . . . and . . . sheep." Paraphrased as "All people that on earth do dwell" and "Before the Lord's eternal throne,"* this psalm has been among the most popular of Christian hymns. The tune written by Louis Bourgeois for the metrical version of Psalm 100, known as Old Hundredth, is perhaps the most familiar hymn tune in Christian hymnody and is said to be the only tune preserved intact from the time of the Reformation.

Christ our Passover

The Canticle, Christ our Passover, was constructed by Archbishop Cranmer for use in the Easter procession; it is made up of passages that proclaim the resurrection found in St. Paul's epistles to the churches in Rome and Corinth. As already stated, *Alleluia* is a shout of praise inherited from the Jewish *Hallelujah* or "praise Yahweh." Christians associate it especially with the celebration of Easter.

*The original line, by John Wesley, was "Before Jehovah's awful throne," but most recent hymnals change the wording somehow because *awful* no longer means "full of awe."

Then follows

The Psalm or Psalms Appointed

At the end of the Psalms is sung or said

Glory to the Father, and to the Son, and to the Holy Spirit: *
   as it was in the beginning, is now, and will be for ever. Amen.

The Lessons

One or two Lessons, as appointed, are read, the Reader first saying

A Reading (Lesson) from _____.

A citation giving chapter and verse may be added.

After each Lesson the Reader may say

              The Word of the Lord.
Answer   Thanks be to God.

Or the Reader may say   Here ends the Lesson (Reading).

Silence may be kept after each Reading. One of the following Canticles, or one of those on pages 47–52 (Canticles 1–7), is sung or said after each Reading. If three Lessons are used, the Lesson from the Gospel is read after the second Canticle.

The Psalm or Psalms Appointed

The psalms are the great hymn book of Judaism and Christianity alike. Many of the most familiar Christian hymns are simply paraphrases of psalms. No poem has been as widely used and loved as Psalm 23; Psalms 1, 15, 95, 100, and 150 are almost as highly valued. The psalms run the gamut of human emotion, from grief and doubt and anger to joy and praise. Regular and frequent use of the psalms makes them part of our vocabulary, available to help us speak to God whatever the need or occasion. Note the directions on pages 582–584 concerning the ways in which the psalms can be said and the importance of making a distinct pause at the asterisk for the sake of rhythm and meaning.

The Lessons

The Lessons are the heart of the Daily Office: God's Word addressing us in a context of prayer and praise. It is a temptation for Christians to select favorite passages rather than read the whole Bible in a disciplined way. The medieval church had gradually shortened the passages read in its services to a few verses at a time, so Cranmer set out to restore the reading of the whole Bible. Revised many times since Cranmer's day, the lectionary (table of readings) still has the same goal. On pages 936–1001, readings are suggested for every day of the year in a two-year cycle and for special occasions as well. Readings assigned to Year One are read in odd-numbered years and those for Year Two are read in even-numbered years. But these selections are also incomplete. Especially if Christians are reading the Office privately, they might find it preferable to read through the Bible a chapter at time, or to read one chapter each of the Old and New Testaments daily, so that they will read the entire Bible and gain context and perspective. Note also that provision is made for reading one, two, or three passages with both Offices.

8   The Song of Moses   *Cantemus Domino*

Exodus 15:1–6, 11–13, 17–18 Especially suitable for use in Easter Season

I will sing to the Lord, for he is lofty and uplifted; *
  the horse and its rider has he hurled into the sea.
The Lord is my strength and my refuge; *
  the Lord has become my Savior.
This is my God and I will praise him, *
  the God of my people and I will exalt him.
The Lord is a mighty warrior; *
  Yahweh is his Name.
The chariots of Pharaoh and his army has he hurled into the sea; *
  the finest of those who bear armor have been
    drowned in the Red Sea.
The fathomless deep has overwhelmed them; *
  they sank into the depths like a stone.
Your right hand, O Lord, is glorious in might; *
  your right hand, O Lord, has overthrown the enemy.
Who can be compared with you, O Lord, among the gods? *
  who is like you, glorious in holiness,
  awesome in renown, and worker of wonders?
You stretched forth your right hand; *
  the earth swallowed them up.
With your constant love you led the people you redeemed; *
  with your might you brought them in safety to
    your holy dwelling.
You will bring them in and plant them *
  on the mount of your possession,
The resting-place you have made for yourself, O Lord, *
  the sanctuary, O Lord, that your hand has established.
The Lord shall reign*
  for ever and for ever.

Glory to the Father, and to the Son, and to the Holy Spirit: *
  as it was in the beginning, is now, and will be for ever. Amen.

Canticles

The reading of each Lesson is followed by a Canticle: this may be an ancient hymn from the Bible or the early church, or even one of the psalms. Fourteen Canticles are provided on pages 85–96, but the traditional-language versions of many of them (pages 47–53) can also be used. A suggested plan for using all the Canticles in turn is provided on page 144. Some of the Canticles are associated with certain seasons, and usually the Old Testament Canticles (8–14) will be more appropriate after the first reading, and the Canticles from the New Testament and early church will fit better after New Testament readings.

The Canticles have a very practical purpose: to provide an intermission and change of pace between the reading of Lessons, to provide opportunity to reflect on the Lessons, and to enable participants to respond to the Lessons with an act of praise.

8 The Song of Moses

The song of victory celebrating the Jewish escape from slavery in Egypt became a part of the Easter Vigil service at an early date and then found its way into other medieval services. Christians have always regarded the passage of Israel through the Red Sea as parallel to their own passage through the waters of baptism into the promised land of the church. Because the 1979 Prayer Book places such stress on the centrality of Easter and baptism, this Canticle was added. It is suggested that this Canticle is most appropriate in Easter Season.

9   The First Song of Isaiah   *Ecce, Deus*
       Isaiah 12:2–6

Surely, it is God who saves me; *
    I will trust in him and not be afraid.
For the Lord is my stronghold and my sure defense, *
    and he will be my Savior.
Therefore you shall draw water with rejoicing *
    from the springs of salvation.
And on that day you shall say, *
    Give thanks to the Lord and call upon his Name;
Make his deeds known among the peoples; *
    see that they remember that his Name is exalted.
Sing the praises of the Lord, for he has done great things, *
    and this is known in all the world.
Cry aloud, inhabitants of Zion, ring out your joy, *
    for the great one in the midst of you is the Holy One of Israel.

Glory to the Father, and to the Son, and to the Holy Spirit: *
    as it was in the beginning, is now, and will be for ever. Amen.

10   The Second Song of Isaiah   *Quœrite Dominum*
       Isaiah 55:6–11

Seek the Lord while he wills to be found; *
call upon him when he draws near.
Let the wicked forsake their ways *
and the evil ones their thoughts;
And let them turn to the Lord, and he will have compassion, *
and to our God, for he will richly pardon.
For my thoughts are not your thoughts, *
nor your ways my ways, says the Lord.
For as the heavens are higher than the earth, *
so are my ways higher than your ways,
and my thoughts than your thoughts.

9, 10, and 11 The First, Second, and Third Songs of Isaiah

These three Canticles (see Glossary) have not been included in any previous version of the Prayer Book (except the Third Song in a recent Canadian Prayer Book) but are found in some medieval and Eastern Office books and liturgies. These are some of the many psalms found not in the Book of Psalms but in one of the prophets. Giving thanks as they do for God's saving strength and victory, they make an appropriate response to many passages from the Bible. Like Canticles 12, 14, 18, and 19, they have been translated by Dr. Charles Guilbert.

12 and 13 A Song of Creation and A Song of Praise

These two Canticles (in reverse order) were later additions to the Book of Daniel and are now found in the Apocrypha (see Glossary). A paraphrase of Psalm 148, these Canticles are said to be have been the song sung by the three men thrown into the fiery furnace by King Nebuchadnezzar (see Daniel 3). They have always been popular among Christians and have been in the Book of Common Prayer since 1549.

14 A Song of Penitence

This Canticle also is from the Apocrypha but was composed to add Manasseh's prayer of repentance to the account in 2 Chronicles 33. It has some previous history of liturgical use but was not in the Book of Common Prayer before 1979. As a prayer of penitence, it is especially appropriate in Lent.

For as rain and snow fall from the heavens *
    and return not again, but water the earth,
Bringing forth life and giving growth, *
    seed for sowing and bread for eating,
So is my word that goes forth from my mouth; *
    it will not return to me empty;
But it will accomplish that which I have purposed, *
    and prosper in that for which I sent it.

Glory to the Father, and to the Son, and to the Holy Spirit: *
    as it was in the beginning, is now, and will be for ever. Amen.

11 The Third Song of Isaiah *Surge, illuminare*
Isaiah 60:1–3, 11a, 14c, 18–19

Arise, shine, for your light has come, *
    and the glory of the Lord has dawned upon you.
For behold, darkness covers the land; *
    deep gloom enshrouds the peoples.
But over you the Lord will rise, *
    and his glory will appear upon you.
Nations will stream to your light, *
    and kings to the brightness of your dawning.
Your gates will always be open; *
    by day or night they will never be shut.
They will call you, The City of the Lord, *
    The Zion of the Holy One of Israel.
Violence will no more be heard in your land, *
    ruin or destruction within your borders.
You will call your walls, Salvation, *
    and all your portals, Praise.
The sun will no more be your light by day; *
    by night you will not need the brightness of the moon.

The Lord will be your everlasting light, *
    and your God will be your glory.

Glory to the Father, and to the Son, and to the Holy Spirit: *
    as it was in the beginning, is now, and will be for ever. Amen.

12   A Song of Creation   *Benedicite, omnia opera Domini*
Song of the Three Young Men, 35–65

*One or more sections of this Canticle may be used. Whatever the selection,
it begins with the Invocation and concludes with the Doxology.*

Invocation

Glorify the Lord, all you works of the Lord, *
    praise him and highly exalt him for ever.
In the firmament of his power, glorify the Lord, *
    praise him and highly exalt him for ever.

I   The Cosmic Order

Glorify the Lord, you angels and all powers of the Lord, *
    O heavens and all waters above the heavens.
Sun and moon and stars of the sky, glorify the Lord, *
    praise him and highly exalt him for ever.

Glorify the Lord, every shower of rain and fall of dew, *
    all winds and fire and heat.
Winter and summer, glorify the Lord, *
    praise him and highly exalt him for ever.

Glorify the Lord, O chill and cold, *
    drops of dew and flakes of snow.
Frost and cold, ice and sleet, glorify the Lord, *
    praise him and highly exalt him for ever.

Glorify the Lord, O nights and days, *
 O shining light and enfolding dark.
Storm clouds and thunderbolts, glorify the Lord, *
 praise him and highly exalt him for ever.

II The Earth and its Creatures

Let the earth glorify the Lord, *
 praise him and highly exalt him for ever.
Glorify the Lord, O mountains and hills,
and all that grows upon the earth, *
 praise him and highly exalt him for ever.

Glorify the Lord, O springs of water, seas, and streams, *
 O whales and all that move in the waters.
All birds of the air, glorify the Lord, *
 praise him and highly exalt him for ever.

Glorify the Lord, O beasts of the wild, *
 and all you flocks and herds.
O men and women everywhere, glorify the Lord, *
 praise him and highly exalt him for ever.

III The People of God

Let the people of God glorify the Lord, *
 praise him and highly exalt him for ever.
Glorify the Lord, O priests and servants of the Lord, *
 praise him and highly exalt him for ever.

Glorify the Lord, O spirits and souls of the righteous, *
 praise him and highly exalt him for ever.
You that are holy and humble of heart, glorify the Lord, *
 praise him and highly exalt him for ever.

Doxology

Let us glorify the Lord: Father, Son, and Holy Spirit; *
   praise him and highly exalt him for ever.
In the firmament of his power, glorify the Lord, *
   praise him and highly exalt him for ever.

13   A Song of Praise   *Benedictus es, Domine*
Song of the Three Young Men, 29–34

Glory to you, Lord God of our fathers; *
   you are worthy of praise; glory to you.
Glory to you for the radiance of your holy Name; *
   we will praise you and highly exalt you for ever.

Glory to you in the splendor of your temple; *
   on the throne of your majesty, glory to you.
Glory to you, seated between the Cherubim; *
   we will praise you and highly exalt you for ever.

Glory to you, beholding the depths; *
   in the high vault of heaven, glory to you.
Glory to you, Father, Son, and Holy Spirit; *
   we will praise you and highly exalt you for ever.

14   A Song of Penitence   *Kyrie Pantokrator*
Prayer of Manasseh, 1–2, 4, 6–7, 11–15

Especially suitable in Lent, and on other penitential occasions

O Lord and Ruler of the hosts of heaven, *
   God of Abraham, Isaac, and Jacob,
   and of all their righteous offspring:
You made the heavens and the earth, *
   with all their vast array.

All things quake with fear at your presence; *
   they tremble because of your power.
But your merciful promise is beyond all measure; *
   it surpasses all that our minds can fathom.
O Lord, you are full of compassion, *
   long-suffering, and abounding in mercy.
You hold back your hand; *
   you do not punish as we deserve.
In your great goodness, Lord,
you have promised forgiveness to sinners, *
   that they may repent of their sin and be saved.
And now, O Lord, I bend the knee of my heart, *
   and make my appeal, sure of your gracious goodness.
I have sinned, O Lord, I have sinned, *
   and I know my wickedness only too well.
Therefore 1 make this prayer to you: *
   Forgive me, Lord, forgive me.
Do not let me perish in my sin, *
   nor condemn me to the depths of the earth.
For you, O Lord, are the God of those who repent, *
   and in me you will show forth your goodness.
Unworthy as I am, you will save me,
in accordance with your great mercy, *
   and I will praise you without ceasing all the days of my life.
For all the powers of heaven sing your praises, *
   and yours is the glory to ages of ages. Amen.

15   The Song of Mary   *Magnificat*
   Luke 1:46–55

My soul proclaims the greatness of the Lord,
my spirit rejoices in God my Savior; *
   for he has looked with favor on his lowly servant.

15 The Song of Mary

This Canticle, known as the *Magnificat*, has a long history of Prayer Book use at Evening Prayer. The English tradition of Evensong has been enriched by many beautiful choral settings of the *Magnificat* and the *Nunc Dimittis*, still sung today in cathedrals and parish churches of England. Although the *Magnificat* is a New Testament Canticle, it is most appropriately used after the Old Testament reading, since it looks forward to the coming of Christ. St. Luke gives it as the song Mary sang when she was told she had been chosen to be the mother of the Savior. It is modeled on Hannah's song (1 Samuel 2) and draws on other Old Testament sources as well.

16 The Song of Zechariah

Drawing again on Old Testament sources, St. Luke composed this Canticle as Zechariah's response of praise to the birth of John the Baptist. Since it has to do with the promise of redemption, it might also be used before a New Testament reading, and the table of suggested Canticles recommends its use in that position on major holy days and Sundays.

17 The Song of Simeon

The third Canticle drawn from St. Luke is Simeon's response to the presentation of Christ in the Temple. It has a long history of use in the evening and has generally been placed after the second lesson at Evening Prayer, since it gives thanks for the fulfillment of God's promise. The 1979 Prayer Book also provides it for Morning Prayer, for Compline, and for the end of the Burial Office.

From this day all generations will call me blessed: *
 the Almighty has done great things for me,
 and holy is his Name.
He has mercy on those who fear him *
 in every generation.
He has shown the strength of his arm, *
 he has scattered the proud in their conceit.
He has cast down the mighty from their thrones, *
 and has lifted up the lowly.
He has filled the hungry with good things, *
 and the rich he has sent away empty.
He has come to the help of his servant Israel, *
 for he has remembered his promise of mercy,
The promise he made to our fathers, *
 to Abraham and his children for ever.

Glory to the Father, and to the Son, and to the Holy Spirit: *
 as it was in the beginning, is now, and will be for ever. Amen.

16   The Song of Zechariah   *Benedictus Dominus Deus*
Luke 1:68–79

Blessed be the Lord, the God of Israel; *
 he has come to his people and set them free.
He has raised up for us a mighty savior, *
 born of the house of his servant David.
Through his holy prophets he promised of old,
that he would save us from our enemies, *
 from the hands of all who hate us.
He promised to show mercy to our fathers *
 and to remember his holy covenant.
This was the oath he swore to our father Abraham, *
 to set us free from the hands of our enemies,
Free to worship him without fear, *
 holy and righteous in his sight
 all the days of our life.

You, my child, shall be called the prophet of the Most High, *
    for you will go before the Lord to prepare his way,
To give his people knowledge of salvation *
    by the forgiveness of their sins.
In the tender compassion of our God *
    the dawn from on high shall break upon us,
To shine on those who dwell in darkness and the
    shadow of death, *
    and to guide our feet into the way of peace.

Glory to the Father, and to the Son, and to the Holy Spirit: *
    as it was in the beginning, is now, and will be for ever. Amen.

17   The Song of Simeon   *Nunc dimittis*
Luke 2:29–32

Lord, you now have set your servant free *
    to go in peace as you have promised;
For these eyes of mine have seen the Savior, *
    whom you have prepared for all the world to see:
A Light to enlighten the nations, *
    and the glory of your people Israel.

Glory to the Father, and to the Son, and to the Holy Spirit: *
    as it was in the beginning, is now, and will be for ever. Amen.

18   A Song to the Lamb   *Dignus es*
Revelation 4: 11; 5:9–10, 13

Splendor and honor and kingly power *
    are yours by right, O Lord our God,
For you created everything that is, *
    and by your will they were created and have their being;

And yours by right, O lamb that was slain, *
   for with your blood you have redeemed for God,
From every family, language, people, and nation, *
   a kingdom of priests to serve our God.

And so, to him who sits upon the throne, *
   and to Christ the lamb,
Be worship and praise, dominion and splendor, *
   for ever and for evermore.

19   The Song of the Redeemed   *Magna et mirabilia*
Revelation 15:3–4

O ruler of the universe, Lord God,
great deeds are they that you have done, *
   surpassing human understanding.
Your ways are ways of righteousness and truth, *
   O King of all the ages.

Who can fail to do you homage, Lord,
and sing the praises of your Name? *
   for you only are the Holy One.
All nations will draw near and fall down before you, *
   because your just and holy works have been revealed.

Glory to the Father, and to the Son, and to the Holy Spirit: *
   as it was in the beginning, is now, and will be for ever. Amen.

20   Glory to God   *Gloria in excelsis*

Glory to God in the highest,
   and peace to his people on earth.

Lord God, heavenly King,
almighty God and Father,

we worship you, we give you thanks,
we praise you for your glory.

Lord Jesus Christ, only Son of the Father,
Lord God, Lamb of God,
you take away the sin of the world:
    have mercy on us;
you are seated at the right hand of the Father:
    receive our prayer.

For you alone are the Holy One,
you alone are the Lord,
you alone are the Most High,
    Jesus Christ,
    with the Holy Spirit,
    in the glory of God the Father. Amen.

21   You are God   *Te Deum laudamus*

You are God: we praise you;
You are the Lord: we acclaim you;
You are the eternal Father:
All creation worships you.
To you all angels, all the powers of heaven,
Cherubim and Seraphim, sing in endless praise:
    Holy, holy, holy Lord, God of power and might,
    heaven and earth are full of your glory .
The glorious company of apostles praise you.
The noble fellowship of prophets praise you.
The white-robed army of martyrs praise you.
Throughout the world the holy Church acclaims you;
    Father, of majesty unbounded,
    your true and only Son, worthy of all worship,
    and the Holy Spirit, advocate and guide.

You, Christ, are the king of glory,
the eternal Son of the Father.
When you became man to set us free
you did not shun the Virgin's womb.
You overcame the sting of death
and opened the kingdom of heaven to all believers.
You are seated at God's right hand in glory.
We believe that you will come and be our judge.
   Come then, Lord, and help your people,
   bought with the price of your own blood,
   and bring us with your saints
   to glory everlasting.

The Apostles' Creed

Officiant and People together, all standing

I believe in God, the Father almighty,
   creator of heaven and earth.
I believe in Jesus Christ, his only Son, our Lord.
   He was conceived by the power of the Holy Spirit
     and born of the Virgin Mary.
   He suffered under Pontius Pilate,
     was crucified, died, and was buried.
   He descended to the dead.
   On the third day he rose again.
   He ascended into heaven,
     and is seated at the right hand of the Father.
   He will come again to judge the living and the dead.
I believe in the Holy Spirit,
   the holy catholic Church,
   the communion of saints,
   the forgiveness of sins,
   the resurrection of the body,
   and the life everlasting. Amen.

18 and 19 A Song to the Lamb and The Song of the Redeemed
Both of these Canticles may have been Christian hymns before they
were made part of the Book of Revelation. They have had only
limited liturgical use and have not been included in previous Prayer
Books. As visions of heavenly praise, they form an appropriate
response to the New Testament readings, especially at festival times.

20 and 21 Glory to God and *Te Deum*
The only nonbiblical Canticles, these can be traced back at least to
the fourth century. The *Gloria* has been an integral part of the Mass
since the Middle Ages, but the first American Prayer Book allowed it
as an option in Morning Prayer. It is especially appropriate at
Christmas time. The *Te Deum* (a nice legend tells us that it was
composed spontaneously by Ambrose and Augustine at Augustine's
baptism) has had various liturgical uses but has often been set to
music for occasions of great triumph, such as a coronation. It is
especially appropriate for Sundays and major holy days.

The Apostles' Creed

Until this point, the only direction given about body position is that
all should kneel for the confession. It is customary in most places to
remain seated for the psalms, Lessons, and often the Canticles. But
all should stand for the Creed, as we move from the passive position
of hearers to the active position of doers. The Creed, in words that
Christians have recited since at least the second century, is our
response to the readings. Although we have no evidence for the
legend that the apostles themselves wrote this Creed, each contribut-
ing one phrase, we can demonstrate that each phrase of this Creed is
directly drawn from the Bible. It summarizes biblical teaching; it
teaches what the apostles taught. The Apostles' Creed has always
been closely associated with baptism: it is an individual's statement
of faith and reminds us always of the commitment made in our
baptism. The Nicene Creed, by contrast, is a corporate statement of
the church's faith and begins with "We believe . . ."

The Prayers

The people stand or kneel

Officiant	The Lord be with you.
People	And also with you.
Officiant	Let us pray.

Officiant and People

Our Father, who art in heaven,
   hallowed be thy Name,
   thy kingdom come,
   thy will be done,
      on earth as it is in heaven.
Give us this day our daily bread.
And forgive us our trespasses,
   as we forgive those
      who trespass against us.
And lead us not into temptation,
   but deliver us from evil.
For thine is the kingdom,
   and the power, and the glory,
   for ever and ever. Amen.

Our Father in heaven,
   hallowed be your Name,
   your kingdom come,
   your will be done,
      on earth as in heaven.
Give us today our daily bread.
Forgive us our sins
   as we forgive those
      who sin against us.
Save us from the time of trial,
   and deliver us from evil.
For the kingdom, the power,
   and the glory are yours,
   now and for ever. Amen.

Then follows one of these sets of Suffrages

A

V.   Show us your mercy, O Lord;
R.   And grant us your salvation.
V.   Clothe your ministers with righteousness;
R.   Let your people sing with joy.
V.   Give peace, O Lord, in all the world;
R.   For only in you can we live in safety.

Just as the Nicene Creed was a late addition to the Eucharist, so the Apostles' Creed was a late addition to the Daily Office. The Christian faith is best expressed not in words but in worship, mission, and service. The Creeds are a useful verbal summary of our faith, but words alone are never enough.

The Prayers

Prayer in the narrow sense is a very minor element in the service of Morning Prayer. The Lord's Prayer and three other brief prayers are the minimum provided, though many other prayers can be added, as indicated on page 101.

The Lord's Prayer is, of course, the basic prayer of Christians and is closely related to the central themes of this service. We hear in Scripture what God has done and has promised; therefore we pray, "your kingdom come, your will be done." We have come to sanctify time; therefore we pray, "Give us today our daily bread." We have come to praise God; therefore we say, "hallowed be your Name . . . For the kingdom, the power, and the glory are yours, now and for ever. Amen."

We do, however, inevitably come before God with an awareness of our needs and a knowledge of God's willingness and ability to provide for us in every way. Therefore it is appropriate to include in the Daily Offices some opportunity to offer petitions, intercessions, and thanksgivings. These may be offered following the Collect for Grace in the form of "authorized intercessions and thanksgivings," but opportunity may also be provided for individuals present to speak aloud or in silence their own concerns and reasons for thankfulness.

V.	Lord, keep this nation under your care;
R.	And guide us in the way of justice and truth.
V.	Let your way be known upon earth;
R.	Your saving health among all nations.
V.	Let not the needy, O Lord, be forgotten;
R.	Nor the hope of the poor be taken away.
V.	Create in us clean hearts, O God;
R.	And sustain us with your Holy Spirit.

B

V.	Save your people, Lord, and bless your inheritance;
R.	Govern and uphold them, now and always.
V.	Day by day we bless you;
R.	We praise your Name for ever.
V.	Lord, keep us from all sin today;
R.	Have mercy on us, Lord, have mercy.
V.	Lord, show us your love and mercy;
R.	For we put our trust in you.
V.	In you, Lord, is our hope;
R.	And we shall never hope in vain.

The Officiant then says one or more of the following Collects

The Collect of the Day

A Collect for Sundays

O God, you make us glad with the weekly remembrance of the glorious resurrection of your Son our Lord: Give us this day such blessing through our worship of you, that the week to come may be spent in your favor; through Jesus Christ our Lord. *Amen.*

The traditional version of the Lord's Prayer is based on the Great Bible of 1539, a revision of the first complete English-language Bible issued in 1535 by Miles Coverdale. This was the version that was included in the first English Prayer Book in 1549 and was too familiar to be replaced by the King James Version when it came out more than sixty years later. Protestant churches, however, generally used the King James Version of 1611 (with "debts" instead of "trespasses") but have recently begun to use the older version more often. The contemporary version is the work of the International Consultation on English Texts (ICET), an ecumenical committee created to provide modern texts that all churches can use in common. (The Song of Zechariah, Glory to God, Song of Mary, and You are God are also the work of the ICET.)

The versicles and responses after the Lord's Prayer are called "suffrages," from a Latin word meaning support or assistance. Suffragan bishop and suffragettes are related words. These brief prayers ask God's help and assistance for ourselves, the church, the world, and those in need. Both sets of suffrages have medieval roots but are drawn (except the fourth versicle and response in set A) from the psalms. They are often called "The Lesser Litany" and are very similar in purpose to the prayers that follow.

A Collect for Fridays

Almighty God, whose most dear Son went not up to joy but first he suffered pain, and entered not into glory before he was crucified: Mercifully grant that we, walking in the way of the cross, may find it none other than the way of life and peace; through Jesus Christ your Son our Lord. *Amen.*

A Collect for Saturdays

Almighty God, who after the creation of the world rested from all your works and sanctified a day of rest for all your creatures: Grant that we, putting away all earthly anxieties, may be duly prepared for the service of your sanctuary, and that our rest here upon earth may be a preparation for the eternal rest promised to your people in heaven; through Jesus Christ our Lord. *Amen.*

A Collect for the Renewal of Life

O God, the King eternal, whose light divides the day from the night and turns the shadow of death into the morning: Drive far from us all wrong desires, incline our hearts to keep your law, and guide our feet into the way of peace; that, having done your will with cheerfulness during the day, we may, when night comes, rejoice to give you thanks; through Jesus Christ our Lord. *Amen.*

A Collect for Peace

O God, the author of peace and lover of concord, to know you is eternal life and to serve you is perfect freedom: Defend us, your humble servants, in all assaults of our enemies; that we, surely trusting in your defense, may not fear the power of any adversaries; through the might of Jesus Christ our Lord. *Amen.*

The Collects and Prayers

A collect (pronounced "coll'-ect") is a brief form of prayer that collects our thoughts around a single theme. The Collect for the Day may be used or one or more of the others. These collects draw on various sources, ranging from St. Augustine (a phrase in the Collect for Peace) to Archbishop Edward White Benson of Canterbury, 1882–1896 (Collect for Saturdays).

Three of these prayers are designated for the last three days of the week but, since there are seven prayers provided, it would be possible to use one in turn each day of the week.

One of three "prayers for mission" follows the collect(s). The first of these is an ancient part of the Good Friday liturgy, while the second was written by a nineteenth-century missionary bishop of Calcutta, and the third by Charles Henry Brent, who served as Bishop of the Philippines (1901–1918) and Western New York (1918–1929).

A hymn or anthem may be sung before the closing prayers. An "Office Hymn" was a usual part of the monastic service and has typically been an optional part of Morning Prayer.

The General Thanksgiving is believed to have been inspired by a private prayer of Queen Elizabeth I and was first included in the 1662 English Prayer Book. Said in unison, it provides a balance to the General Confession said at the beginning of the service. Its beautifully shaped phrases have made it one of the best-known and loved prayers in the Prayer Book. "The means of grace and . . . the hope of glory" is a powerful summary of the effects of Christ's ministry. The prayer moves from thankfulness for God's gifts to the need to give ourselves to God's service as we go out from this time of prayer.

A Collect for Grace

Lord God, almighty and everlasting Father, you have brought us in safety to this new day: Preserve us with your mighty power, that we may not fall into sin, nor be overcome by adversity; and in all we do, direct us to the fulfilling of your purpose; through Jesus Christ our Lord. *Amen.*

A Collect for Guidance

Heavenly Father, in you we live and move and have our being: We humbly pray you so to guide and govern us by your Holy Spirit, that in all the cares and occupations of our life we may not forget you, but may remember that we are ever walking in your sight; through Jesus Christ our Lord. *Amen.*

Then, unless the Eucharist or a form of general intercession is to follow, one of these prayers for mission is added

Almighty and everlasting God, by whose Spirit the whole body of your faithful people is governed and sanctified: Receive our supplications and prayers which we offer before you for all members of your holy Church, that in their vocation and ministry they may truly and devoutly serve you; through our Lord and Savior Jesus Christ. *Amen.*

or this

O God, you have made of one blood all the peoples of the earth, and sent your blessed Son to preach peace to those who are far off and to those who are near: Grant that people everywhere may seek after you and find you; bring the nations into your fold; pour out your Spirit upon all flesh; and hasten the coming of your kingdom; through Jesus Christ our Lord. *Amen.*

or the following

Lord Jesus Christ, you stretched out your arms of love on
the hard wood of the cross that everyone might come within
the reach of your saving embrace: So clothe us in your Spirit
that we, reaching forth our hands in love, may bring those
who do not know you to the knowledge and love of you; for
the honor of your Name. *Amen.*

Here may be sung a hymn or anthem.

Authorized intercessions and thanksgivings may follow.

Before the close of the Office one or both of the following may be used

The General Thanksgiving

Officiant and People

Almighty God, Father of all mercies,
we your unworthy servants give you humble thanks
for all your goodness and loving-kindness
to us and to all whom you have made.
We bless you for our creation, preservation,
and all the blessings of this life;
but above all for your immeasurable love
in the redemption of the world by our Lord Jesus Christ;
for the means of grace, and for the hope of glory.
And, we pray, give us such an awareness of your mercies,
that with truly thankful hearts we may show forth your praise,
not only with our lips, but in our lives,
by giving up our selves to your service,
and by walking before you
in holiness and righteousness all our days;
through Jesus Christ our Lord,
to whom, with you and the Holy Spirit,
be honor and glory throughout all ages. Amen.

A Prayer of St. Chrysostom

Almighty God, you have given us grace at this time with one accord to make our common supplication to you; and you have promised through your well-beloved Son that when two or three are gathered together in his Name you will be in the midst of them: Fulfill now, O Lord, our desires and petitions as may be best for us; granting us in this world knowledge of your truth, and in the age to come life everlasting. *Amen.*

Then may be said

Let us bless the Lord.
Thanks be to God.

From Easter Day through the Day of Pentecost "Alleluia, alleluia" may be added to the preceding versicle and response.

The Officiant may then conclude with one of the following

The grace of our Lord Jesus Christ, and the love of God, and the fellowship of the Holy Spirit, be with us all evermore.
Amen.   *2 Corinthians 13:14*

May the God of hope fill us with all joy and peace in believing through the power of the Holy Spirit.   *Amen.*   *Romans 15:13*

Glory to God whose power, working in us, can do infinitely more than we can ask or imagine: Glory to him from generation to generation in the Church, and in Christ Jesus for ever and ever. *Amen.*
Ephesians 3:20, 21

A Prayer of St. Chrysostom (who died in the year 407 CE) probably does not go back quite that far but has been used in the Greek liturgy from a very early date. It is based on Jesus' teaching in Matthew 18:20 and, recalling Jesus' promise of God's response to prayer, it forms a fitting conclusion to the prayers that have been offered.

"Let us bless the Lord," with the response "Thanks be to God," is a traditional conclusion of many services and is an option at the end of the Eucharist as well.

As the service began, so it concludes with a verse from the Bible. Each of the three choices offered comes from one of the Epistles of St. Paul, either where it concludes the Epistle itself (2 Corinthians) or in the main body of his teaching (the Epistles to the Romans and Ephesians). Only the first sentence refers to the Trinity but the other two speak more specifically of the power at work within us to give joy and peace and to accomplish God's purpose.

Part II
Daily Evening Prayer

Daily Evening Prayer: Rite Two

The Officiant begins the service with one or more of the following sentences of Scripture, or of those on pages 75–78;

or with the Service of Light on pages 109–112, and continuing with the appointed Psalmody;

or with the versicle "O God, make speed to save us" on page 117.

Let my prayer be set forth in your sight as incense, the lifting up of my hands as the evening sacrifice.   *Psalm 141:2*

Grace to you and peace from God our Father and from the Lord Jesus Christ.   *Philippians 1:2*

Worship the Lord in the beauty of holiness; let the whole earth tremble before him.   *Psalm 96:9*

Yours is the day, O God, yours also the night; you established the moon and the sun. You fixed all the boundaries of the earth; you made both summer and winter.   *Psalm 74: 15, 16*

I will bless the Lord who gives me counsel; my heart teaches me, night after night. I have set the Lord always before me; because he is at my right hand, I shall not fall.   *Psalm 16: 7, 8*

Seek him who made the Pleiades and Orion, and turns deep darkness into the morning, and darkens the day into night; who calls for the waters of the sea and pours them out upon the surface of the earth: The Lord is his name.   *Amos 5:8*

Commentary

As in the case of Morning Prayer, the first difference between Evening Prayer Rite I and Rite II is one of traditional and contemporary language. Evening Prayer Rite I, however, differs even less from the Rite II version than does Morning Prayer Rite I from Rite II. Aside from the language, the only other difference is that the traditional version of the General Confession is provided in Rite I with the phrasing slightly modified from that of the 1928 Prayer Book; the phrases, "and there is no health in us" and "miserable sinners," are omitted.

Much of the service of Evening Prayer is often sung, so it is commonly known as "Evensong." The text of the service may be sung to plainsong, Anglican chant, or more elaborate choral settings. In this form, it is a very popular service in England and in a few places in the United States as well. The simple "said" service as set out here, however, may be prayed by an individual at home or in any quiet place and, as with Daily Morning Prayer, provides a way to set each day in a context of prayer and praise.

The offices for the morning and evening are very similar in structure and it has often been suggested that they be combined into one office to be used at either time. The services in their present form, however, do provide different themes and thoughts appropriate to the time of day. The similarity of structure simply makes it more convenient for those using the services to learn and use them both.

The directions for saying Morning Prayer (Prayer Book, page 75) apply to Evening Prayer as well. The Office may be said by anyone, ordained or not, and it is recommended that people other than the leader read the Lessons. Evening Prayer may also replace the first part of the Eucharist.

Opening Sentences

The Opening Sentences provided here are all general in nature, though several make specific reference to the theme of darkness and light. For sentences to mark a particular season, those provided for Morning Prayer may be used. The Service of Light (pages 109–112) may also be used as an opening.

There are three other ways to begin the service. The Opening Sentences may be followed by the General Confession or by the Invitatory and Psalter at pages 117–118. The Opening Sentences may also be omitted for the service to begin with the Invitatory. Thus the emphasis may be placed on the time of day, the theme of penitence, or the praise of God.

If I say, "Surely the darkness will cover me, and the light around me turn to night," darkness is not dark to you, O Lord; the night is as bright as the day; darkness and light to you are both alike.
Psalm 139:10, 11

Jesus said, "I am the light of the world; whoever follows me will not walk in darkness, but will have the light of life."
John 8:12

The following Confession of Sin may then be said; or the Office may continue at once with "O God, make speed to save us."

Confession of Sin

The Officiant says to the people

Dear friends in Christ, here in the presence of Almighty God,
let us kneel in silence, and with penitent and obedient hearts confess
our sins, so that we may obtain forgiveness by his
infinite goodness and mercy.

or this

Let us confess our sins against God and our neighbor.

Silence may be kept.

Officiant and People together, all kneeling

Most merciful God,
we confess that we have sinned against you
in thought, word, and deed,
by what we have done,
and by what we have left undone.
We have not loved you with our whole heart;
we have not loved our neighbors as ourselves.
We are truly sorry and we humbly repent.

Confession of Sin

In the first English Book of Common Prayer and all Prayer Books until the American revision of 1892, the service began with sentences of Scripture that emphasized human sinfulness, immediately followed by a Confession of Sin. Modern study of the origins of Christian worship, however, has led to a general agreement that the first Christians placed the emphasis on thankfulness and praise. Because of that understanding, the directions for Evening Prayer have been revised to allow the service to begin on a note of praise by omitting the confession. The Daily Offices, after all, are primarily a means of reading and reflecting on the Scriptures and are not intended to focus on the need for forgiveness, which might more appropriately be dealt with daily in private prayer. Individuals or congregations might prefer to make it a rule to begin with the confession on Fridays or in Lent. In those cases, they might begin with the penitential sentences provided for Morning Prayer.

Opportunity for silence should always be provided before the confession so that it is not said casually or thoughtlessly.

Notice also that the confession is a "general" one, speaking of sins of thought, word, and deed, omission and commission, and failures in our relationships with others. The silence should be used to recall specifics of our own lives so that these may be offered within the general words.

The Absolution

The priest may pronounce God's forgiveness or a lay person may pray for it; in either event, the absolution goes on to ask for strength to continue in relationship with God and for the Holy Spirit to keep us within that eternal relationship.

For the sake of your Son Jesus Christ,
have mercy on us and forgive us;
that we may delight in your will,
and walk in your ways,
to the glory of your Name. Amen.

The Priest alone stands and says

Almighty God have mercy on you, forgive you all your
sins through our Lord Jesus Christ, strengthen you in all
goodness, and by the power of the Holy Spirit keep you in
eternal life. *Amen.*

The Invitatory and Psalter

All stand

Officiant   O God, make speed to save us.
People   O Lord, make haste to help us.

Officiant and People

Glory to the Father, and to the Son, and to the Holy Spirit: as
it was in the beginning, is now, and will be for ever. Amen.

Except in Lent, add   Alleluia.

*The following, or some other suitable hymn, or an Invitatory Psalm, may be
sung or said*

The Invitatory and Psalter

As in Morning Prayer, verses from the psalms are used as a prelude to the reading of the psalms, to invite our participation, and to provide a seasonal setting.

The opening verse and response from Psalm 70 were a part of the pre-Reformation English office and are still a part of the English Prayer Book. They were dropped from the first American Prayer Book (in favor of the opening verse and response from Morning Prayer: "O Lord, open our lips") but restored in 1979. The *Gloria Patri* follows, with the *Alleluia*, except during Lent.

O Gracious Light   *Phos hilaron*

O gracious Light,
pure brightness of the everliving Father in heaven,
O Jesus Christ, holy and blessed!

Now as we come to the setting of the sun,
and our eyes behold the vesper light,
we sing your praises, O God: Father, Son, and Holy Spirit.

You are worthy at all times to be praised by happy voices,
O Son of God, O Giver of Life,
and to be glorified through all the worlds.

Then follows

The Psalm or Psalms Appointed

At the end of the Psalms is sung or said

Glory to the Father, and to the Son, and to the Holy Spirit: *
  as it was in the beginning, is now, and will be for ever. Amen.

The Lessons

One or two Lessons, as appointed, are read, the Reader first saying

A Reading (Lesson) from —————.

A citation giving chapter and verse may be added.

O Gracious Light

The *Phos hilaron* is a hymn so old that St. Basil spoke of it as a cherished tradition in 379 CE. The singing of a hymn was a traditional part of the medieval offices but the *Phos hilaron* was not part of the English tradition. The version provided here was written for the 1979 Prayer Book. There are metrical versions of the *Phos hilaron* that might also be used. As daylight fades, the hymn praises Jesus Christ in whom human beings came to see the light of God.

The Psalms

The Daily Office Lectionary at the back of the Prayer Book (pages 934–1001) provides two sets of psalms for each day, one for the morning and one for the evening. Following that plan, it is possible to read all the psalms over a seven-week period. The Psalter is also divided into sixty segments so that it can be read through each month. The psalms will most often set a tone of praise here at the beginning of the office; the Lectionary generally assigns penitential psalms to Fridays.

The Lessons

The Lectionary (BCP pages 936–1001) provides three readings for each day—two for the morning and one for the evening. It further suggests that the Gospel reading be used in the evening of Year One and in the morning of Year Two. If those using the Offices prefer to use two readings at each service, they can draw a second Old Testament reading from the alternate year's lectionary. It is even possible to use a third reading after the second Canticle and before the Creed. Whatever arrangement is chosen, the point is to be able to read through the Bible in a logical way.

Silence

A time of silence should follow each reading. The point of reading the Bible is to allow God's word to sink in and be applied to each individual's life and the whole of life. Silence provides a time to ask, "What does this Scripture say to me? What impact should it have on my life? How does it help me to understand God's will more clearly?"

After each Lesson the Reader may say

> The Word of the Lord.
Answer   Thanks be to God.

Or the Reader may say   Here ends the Lesson (Reading).

Silence may be kept after each Reading. One of the following Canticles, or one of those on pages 47–52, or 85–95, is sung or said after each Reading. If three Lessons are used, the Lesson from the Gospel is read after the second Canticle.

The Song of Mary   *Magnificat*

Luke 1:46–55

My soul proclaims the greatness of the Lord,
my spirit rejoices in God my Savior; *
   for he has looked with favor on his lowly servant.
From this day all generations will call me blessed: *
   the Almighty has done great things for me,
   and holy is his Name.
He has mercy on those who fear him *
   in every generation.
He has shown the strength of his arm, *
   he has scattered the proud in their conceit.
He has cast down the mighty from their thrones, *
   and has lifted up the lowly.
He has filled the hungry with good things, *
   and the rich he has sent away empty.
He has come to the help of his servant Israel, *
   for he has remembered his promise of mercy,
The promise he made to our fathers, *
   to Abraham and his children for ever.

Glory to the Father, and to the Son, and to the Holy Spirit: *
   as it was in the beginning, is now, and will be for ever. Amen.

Canticles

The Song of Mary, or *Magnificat*

In the great English tradition of Evensong, the Canticles traditionally sung are always the *Magnificat* and *Nunc Dimittis*, for which many of the best-known composers have provided settings. These Canticles can also be sung to the ancient plainsong modes or Anglican Chant, which are designed to fit lines of variant length, or to hymn tunes if metrical versions of the texts are used.

Note that the various Canticles provided for Morning Prayer can also be used in the evening.

The *Magnificat* appropriately follows the Old Testament reading, since it offers praise for what God has done in the past "in every generation" and looks forward to the working out of God's purpose in the birth of Jesus. St. Luke, in whose version of the Gospel this song is found, gives special attention in his writing to the role of women in Jesus' life and to Jesus' concern for the poor and outcast, interests that are very prominent in the *Magnificat*. The Canticle proclaims God's revolutionary role in human life, throwing down those who trust in their wealth and accomplishments and raising up those who have been less favored in material terms.

The Canticle also reminds us of the central role of Mary in God's plan of salvation, a role that became controversial when it was overemphasized in the Western church and therefore downplayed or eliminated by some reformed traditions. A familiar hymn speaks of Mary as "Higher than the Seraphim, more glorious than the Cherubim . . . bearer of the eternal word, most glorious . . ." Her response of humble acceptance ("Let it be with me according to your word") to the angel's announcement of her role remains a model for all Christian response to God's will.

The Song of Simeon *Nunc dimittis*

Luke 2:29–32

Lord, you now have set your servant free *
  to go in peace as you have promised;
For these eyes of mine have seen the Savior, *
  whom you have prepared for all the world to see:
A Light to enlighten the nations, *
  and the glory of your people Israel.

Glory to the Father, and to the Son, and to the Holy Spirit: *
  as it was in the beginning, is now, and will be for ever. Amen.

The Apostles' Creed

Officiant and People together, all standing

I believe in God, the Father almighty,
  creator of heaven and earth.
I believe in Jesus Christ, his only Son, our Lord.
  He was conceived by the power of the Holy Spirit
    and born of the Virgin Mary.
  He suffered under Pontius Pilate,
    was crucified, died, and was buried.
  He descended to the dead.
  On the third day he rose again.
  He ascended into heaven,
    and is seated at the right hand of the Father.
  He will come again to judge the living and the dead.
I believe in the Holy Spirit,
  the holy catholic Church,
  the communion of saints,
  the forgiveness of sins,
  the resurrection of the body,
  and the life everlasting. Amen.

Song of Simeon, or *Nunc Dimittis*

The second traditional Canticle of Evening Prayer or Evensong is the Song of Simeon, also known by its Latin title, *Nunc Dimittis*. In the Gospel according to St. Luke, this song was sung by Simeon, described by Luke as an elderly resident of Jerusalem who had been promised that he would live to see the Messiah. When Jesus' parents brought their baby to the temple to make the traditional offering in thanksgiving for the birth of the first male child, Simeon met them and said the words we repeat at Evening Prayer today. As the *Magnificat* reflects on what God has done in the past, so the *Nunc Dimittis* looks forward to what God will do in bringing the light of the knowledge of God's glory to all nations.

A sermon or homily may be placed after the readings and before the Creed.

The Apostles' Creed

The Apostles' Creed is an appropriate response of faith that flows from the readings of Scripture: what we have heard is what we believe. The Apostles' Creed comes from the earliest period of Christian history and was first used as a statement of faith at baptism. Like the Nicene Creed used at the Eucharist, it has three primary sections affirming faith in the Triune God, but by far the largest part is given to the summary of Jesus' life, death, ascension, and presence at the Father's right hand. Our worship, like our faith, is centered on Christ, in whom God is fully revealed to us and through whom we are brought back into union with God.

The Apostles' Creed is omitted if the Eucharist is to follow.

The Prayers

The people stand or kneel

Officiant   The Lord be with you.
People   And also with you.
Officiant   Let us pray.

Officiant and People

Our Father, who art in heaven,
  hallowed be thy Name,
  thy kingdom come,
  thy will be done,
    on earth as it is in heaven.
Give us this day our daily bread.
And forgive us our trespasses,
  as we forgive those
    who trespass against us.
And lead us not into temptation,
  but deliver us from evil.
For thine is the kingdom,
  and the power, and the glory,
  for ever and ever. Amen.

Our Father in heaven,
  hallowed be your Name,
  your kingdom come,
  your will be done,
    on earth as in heaven.
Give us today our daily bread.
Forgive us our sins
  as we forgive those
    who sin against us.
Save us from the time of trial,
  and deliver us from evil.
For the kingdom, the power,
  and the glory are yours,
  now and for ever. Amen.

Then follows one of these sets of Suffrages

A

V.   Show us your mercy, O Lord;
R.   And grant us your salvation.
V.   Clothe your ministers with righteousness;
R.   Let your people sing with joy.
V.   Give peace, O Lord, in all the world;
R.   For only in you can we live in safety.

The Prayers

Having praised God and heard the Scriptures read, the remainder of the service is an offering of prayer and begins with the Lord's Prayer, the model of all Christian prayer. As always in the Book of Common Prayer, the traditional version and modern version are available. Used here to mark the transition to the time of prayer is the traditional verse and response: "The Lord be with you. And also with you. Let us pray."

V.	Lord, keep this nation under your care;
R.	And guide us in the way of justice and truth.
V.	Let your way be known upon earth;
R.	Your saving health among all nations.
V.	Let not the needy, O Lord, be forgotten;
R.	Nor the hope of the poor be taken away.
V.	Create in us clean hearts, O God;
R.	And sustain us with your Holy Spirit.

B

That this evening may be holy, good, and peaceful,
We entreat you, O Lord.

That your holy angels may lead us in paths of peace and goodwill,
We entreat you, O Lord.

That we may be pardoned and forgiven for our sins and offenses,
We entreat you, O Lord.

That there may be peace to your Church and to the whole world,
We entreat you, O Lord.

That we may depart this life in your faith and fear, and not be condemned before the great judgment seat of Christ,
We entreat you, O Lord.

That we may be bound together by your Holy Spirit in the communion of [———and] all your saints, entrusting one another and all our life to Christ,
We entreat you, O Lord.

The Officiant then says one or more of the following Collects

The Collect of the Day

The Suffrages

The Lord's Prayer is followed by a short litany composed, for the most part, of verses from the psalms. The series of verses can also be seen as a compact intercessory prayer, moving from a petition for mercy and salvation through prayer for the clergy, the laity, this nation, all nations, and the poor and needy. The final petition is similar to the Collect for Purity with which the Eucharist often begins, asking for the cleanness of heart and guidance of the Holy Spirit that are the essential foundations of all prayer.

The suffrages are often sung to a simple plainsong tone but may also be sung to more elaborate settings by a choir.

Suffrages B

The second set of suffrages is new to the 1979 Prayer Book and comes from the Evening service of the Eastern Orthodox churches. The concerns expressed are very similar to those of the first set of suffrages but with a greater emphasis on pardon, peace, and forgiveness, and on the unseen spiritual forces surrounding us: the holy angels and communion of saints.

These suffrages also may be sung to a simple plainsong setting.

A Collect for Sundays

Lord God, whose Son our Savior Jesus Christ triumphed over the powers of death and prepared for us our place in the new Jerusalem: Grant that we, who have this day given thanks for his resurrection, may praise you in that City of which he is the light, and where he lives and reigns for ever and ever. *Amen.*

A Collect for Fridays

Lord Jesus Christ, by your death you took away the sting of death: Grant to us your servants so to follow in faith where you have led the way, that we may at length fall asleep peacefully in you and wake up in your likeness; for your tender mercies' sake. *Amen.*

A Collect for Saturdays

O God, the source of eternal light: Shed forth your unending day upon us who watch for you, that our lips may praise you, our lives may bless you, and our worship on the morrow give you glory; through Jesus Christ our Lord. *Amen.*

A Collect for Peace

Most holy God, the source of all good desires, all right judgments, and all just works: Give to us, your servants, that peace which the world cannot give, so that our minds may be fixed on the doing of your will, and that we, being delivered from the fear of all enemies, may live in peace and quietness; through the mercies of Christ Jesus our Savior. *Amen.*

A Collect for Aid against Perils

Be our light in the darkness, O Lord, and in your great mercy defend us from all perils and dangers of this night; for the love of your only Son, our Savior Jesus Christ. *Amen.*

The Collects

As at Morning Prayer, seven collects are provided—not counting the Collect of the Day, which is not printed here but would allow a different collect to be used each day. The first three collects are assigned to the first and last two days of the week and are new to the 1979 Prayer Book.

The Collect for Sundays was composed by William Bright, a nineteenth-century English priest and one of the great authors and translators of prayer in the Anglican tradition. Since Sunday is always a celebration of the resurrection and looks forward to eternal life, the collect draws its imagery and its vision of a new Jerusalem from Revelation 21.

The Collect for Fridays, the day of Jesus' death, is again from a late-nineteenth-century source and was included in the 1892 American Prayer Book in the Burial Office. It is also in the 1979 Prayer Book as a prayer for use at funerals. It makes reference to passages in three of St. Paul's Epistles (Romans 6:5; 1 Corinthians 15:17–19, 54–57; 1 Thessalonians 4:14–15) as well as to John 14:6.

The Collect for Saturdays is based on a prayer in the Sarum Breviary, a pre-Reformation English Prayer Book, and contains themes appropriate to the eve of Sunday, with its references to "eternal light" and "unending day."

The Collect for Peace and the Collect for Aid against Perils, both from a seventh-century source, were both fixed parts of the Evening Office until the 1979 Prayer Book.

The Collect for Peace reminds us of the way "holy desires" lead us to make "right judgments" that enable us to perform "just works," but that God is the source of all. The Collect then prays for the peace beyond what the world can give that enables us to fix our minds on doing God's will.

The Collect for Aid against Perils comes from an age when the night was undiluted by the artificial light that makes it hard for us to see the stars today. In this darkness, the world was a more dangerous place. Artificial light, however, does nothing to lighten the darkness of ignorance and the rejection of God's will. We need to pray for God's light to shine on us at all times, not just at night.

A Collect for Protection

O God, the life of all who live, the light of the faithful, the strength of those who labor, and the repose of the dead: We thank you for the blessings of the day that is past, and humbly ask for your protection through the coming night. Bring us in safety to the morning hours; through him who died and rose again for us, your Son our Savior Jesus Christ. *Amen.*

A Collect for the Presence of Christ

Lord Jesus, stay with us, for evening is at hand and the day is past; be our companion in the way, kindle our hearts, and awaken hope, that we may know you as you are revealed in Scripture and the breaking of bread. Grant this for the sake of your love. *Amen.*

Then, unless the Eucharist or a form of general intercession is to follow, one of these prayers for mission is added

O God and Father of all, whom the whole heavens adore: Let the whole earth also worship you, all nations obey you, all tongues confess and bless you, and men and women everywhere love you and serve you in peace; through Jesus Christ our Lord. *Amen.*

or this

Keep watch, dear Lord, with those who work, or watch, or weep this night, and give your angels charge over those who sleep. Tend the sick, Lord Christ; give rest to the weary, bless the dying, soothe the suffering, pity the afflicted, shield the joyous; and all for your love's sake. *Amen.*

or the following

A Collect for Protection

This collect illustrates the way in which prayers may be built up and reworked in successive ages and by different authors. Late in the nineteenth century, William Reed Huntington composed this prayer from phrases in William Bright's translations of early Latin collects.

A Collect for the Presence of Christ

This collect comes from a modern Roman Catholic source, the Breviary of Paul VI, and draws its inspiration from the story in St. Luke's Gospel of the meeting of Jesus with two disciples on the road to Emmaus on Easter Day.

The 1979 Prayer Book frequently gives increased importance to prayer for mission. In both Morning and Evening Prayer, there is always to be a prayer for mission, whether in the three prayers provided or within a general intercession. If the Eucharist is to follow, these prayers may be omitted, since the Prayers of the People would include prayer for mission.

The three prayers for mission come from widely different sources. The first comes from an anonymous collection of prayers published in 1933, the second from the writings of St. Augustine of Hippo in the fifth century, and the last is a revised version of one of William Bright's translations of an early Latin collect.

A hymn or anthem is a traditional part of Evensong "after the third collect," and may be placed here.

The statement that "authorized intercessions and thanksgivings may follow" would suggest that they are to be read from the Prayer Book or other authorized sources and a wide variety of prayers for many purposes is provided in the Book of Common Prayer on pages 814 to 835. One of the "Additional Directions" at the end of this section of the Prayer Book (page 142) does, however, say that opportunity is to be given to members of the congregation to add their own "intentions or objects of prayer."

O God, you manifest in your servants the signs of your
presence: Send forth upon us the Spirit of love, that in
companionship with one another your abounding grace may
increase among us; through Jesus Christ our Lord. *Amen.*

Here may be sung a hymn or anthem.

Authorized intercessions and thanksgivings may follow.

Before the close of the Office one or both of the following may be used

The General Thanksgiving

Officiant and People

Almighty God, Father of all mercies,
we your unworthy servants give you humble thanks
for all your goodness and loving-kindness
to us and to all whom you have made.
We bless you for our creation, preservation,
and all the blessings of this life;
but above all for your immeasurable love
in the redemption of the world by our Lord Jesus Christ;
for the means of grace, and for the hope of glory.
And, we pray, give us such an awareness of your mercies,
that with truly thankful hearts we may show forth your praise,
not only with our lips, but in our lives,
by giving up our selves to your service,
and by walking before you
in holiness and righteousness all our days;
through Jesus Christ our Lord,
to whom, with you and the Holy Spirit,
be honor and glory throughout all ages. Amen.

It is also possible to conclude the service at this point with one of the Scripture verses on page 126.

The General Thanksgiving has been discussed where it occurs at Morning Prayer on page 101. Other general and occasional thanks-givings that might be used here are provided on pages 836 to 841.

A Prayer of St. Chrysostom

Almighty God, you have given us grace at this time with one accord to make our common supplication to you; and you have promised through your well-beloved Son that when two or three are gathered together in his Name you will be in the midst of them: Fulfill now, O Lord, our desires and petitions as may be best for us; granting us in this world knowledge of your truth, and in the age to come life everlasting. *Amen.*

Then may be said

Let us bless the Lord.
Thanks be to God.

From Easter Day through the Day of Pentecost "Alleluia, alleluia" may be added to the preceding versicle and response.

The Officiant may then conclude with one of the following

The grace of our Lord Jesus Christ, and the love of God, and the fellowship of the Holy Spirit, be with us all evermore. *Amen.*   *2 Corinthians 13:14*

May the God of hope fill us with all joy and peace in believing through the power of the Holy Spirit. *Amen.* *Romans 15:13*

Glory to God whose power, working in us, can do infinitely more than we can ask or imagine: Glory to him from generation to generation in the Church, and in Christ Jesus for ever and ever. *Amen.*   *Ephesians 3:20, 21*

The Prayer of St. Chrysostom and the closing sentences of Scripture have been discussed in the section on Morning Prayer, page 27 above.

Glossary

Absolution: To absolve is to set free, so in the Prayer Book the absolution is the declaration by the priest or bishop that those who have confessed their sins are set free from those sins.

Alleluia: This is the English version of the word *Hallelujah* and is a Hebrew word meaning "Praise God." The word is used most often in the Easter Season and is not used at all in Lent.

Anthem: An Anglicized form of the word *antiphon*, the word is now ordinarily used for music sung by a choir. Anthems are often sung during the offertory or after the third collect in the Daily Office.

Antiphon: Sentences, usually from Scripture, said or sung before and after the psalms and Canticles in the Daily Offices.

Antiphonal: A method of reciting the psalms in which verses are said or sung alternately by two groups.

Apocrypha: The word comes from a Greek word meaning "hidden." The apocryphal books of the Bible were not written in Hebrew and therefore were not included in the Hebrew Bible. They were, nonetheless, part of the Bible used in the Greek-speaking world and therefore known and used by the early Christian Church. At the time of the Reformation, these books were excluded from the Bible, though most of them were included by Luther as an appendix. The Church of England included them in the Bible separately from other Old Testament books and said they were not to be used to establish doctrine.

Bidding: A bidding is an invitation to join in a prayer. It is most often used before a Confession of Sin or a general intercession.

Canticle: The word comes from the Latin word for "song." Canticles are texts used in the Daily Offices and drawn from biblical and postbiblical sources.

Chrysostom, St. John (c. 347–407): Patriarch of Constantinople and a great orator. The word *chrysostom* means "silver-tongued." He was often exiled because of his plain speaking about corruption in the church and court. The so-called "Prayer of St. Chrysostom" was probably composed after his death. Cranmer discovered it in the Greek liturgy and brought it into the Prayer Book.

Collect: A short form of prayer (pronounced "coll'-ect") with an invocation, petition, and ascription. Although the accent is on the first syllable in church use, the word has the same meaning as the ordinary word *collect* with the accent on the second syllable. This type of prayer "collects" the thoughts of the congregation into a single theme. The term is most often used for the theme-setting prayer that comes before the Lessons in the Eucharist.

Compline: The last of the ancient monastic offices, it was included in the 1979 Prayer Book.

Cranmer, Thomas (1489–1556): Archbishop of Canterbury during the years when the English Church regained its independence from the Church of Rome. Cranmer edited the first English-language Prayer Book and wrote many of its best-known prayers.

Creed: A statement of faith. The word comes from the Latin *credo*, which means "I believe." The shorter Apostles' Creed is a personal statement and is therefore used at baptisms. The longer Nicene Creed is a corporate statement beginning, therefore, with the word "we."

Direct recitation: In this method of saying the psalms, they are sung or said in unison.

Gloria in excelsis: An expanded version of the song sung by the angels announcing the birth of Christ. It has been used at least since the fourth century. It begins with the words, "Glory to God in the highest."

Gloria Patri: An ascription of praise added to the psalms as early as the fourth century. It begins with the words, "Glory be to the Father."

Hymn: Hymns are the poetry of the Christian church set to music for use in worship.

Intercession: This is prayer offered on behalf of others and is part of almost all Christian worship.

Invitatory: The Canticle at the beginning of the first Office of the day that invites to prayer. The original Invitatory Canticle was Psalm 95 but others are now used as well.

Lauds: The traditional morning office of the Western church, the word means "praise."

Lesson: This term refers to readings from the Bible used in church services. The "First Reading" is usually from the Old Testament, while a "Second Reading" (or sometimes a "Third Reading") is from the New Testament.

Liturgy: The Greek word means "public work." The worship of God is the public work of Christians and all formal worship can be referred to as liturgy. Often the term is used specifically in relation to the Eucharist.

Matins: The midnight office of monastic orders, it was combined with Prime by Cranmer to form Morning Prayer, and the title is often still used for that service.

None: The monastic office for the ninth hour. Pronounced like "known," the word comes from the Latin for "nine."

Office: One of the daily round of monastic or Prayer Book services composed primarily of psalms, readings, and prayers. The word is derived from the Latin word for "duty."

Prime: The monastic office appointed for the first hour of the day or 6 a.m.

Psalter: The Book of Psalms in the Old Testament, but the term is more often used to refer to separate collections of psalms, such as the one included in the Book of Common Prayer.

Responsive recitation: This is probably the most common method of saying the psalms in the Episcopal Church: the leader and congregation alternate saying the verses or half verses.

Responsorial recitation: One of four methods of reciting the psalms recommended in the Prayer Book (page 582). In this method, psalms are sung by a solo voice while choir and congregation sing a refrain.

Rite (ritual): The usual pattern of words used in a service. So the prayers used at the Eucharist are the Eucharistic Rite. The word is often misused to refer to the ceremonies that accompany the words.

Season: The Church Year is divided into seasons, most of which are centered on the life of Christ. The year begins with Advent, the four weeks before Christmas, in which the theme is the "coming" of Christ. Christmas season, the birth of Christ, is followed by Epiphany, the "showing forth" of Christ. Lent is the season of penitence before Easter, which celebrates the resurrection of Jesus from death. The remaining half of the church year is called "Pentecost" and centers on the life and teaching of Jesus.

Sext: Derived from the Latin word for "six," this is the monastic office for the sixth hour of the day, or noon.

Suffrages: These are prayers of intercession, most often the brief prayers like a short Litany toward the end of the Daily Office.

Te Deum **(You, O God):** A great hymn of praise often sung on festival occasions. It is thought to have been written by Niceta, the Bishop of Remesiana in Serbia in the early fifth century.

Terce: Derived from the Latin word for "three," this is the monastic office for the third hour of the day.

Venite: The Latin name for Psalm 95, taken from its first word, "Come." In the Prayer Book it is sometimes shortened and in former Prayer Books has also included verses 9 and 13 of Psalm 96.

Vespers: The monastic office traditionally recited late in the afternoon or just after dark.

Vigil: A nighttime service, often ending with the Eucharist, before a Sunday or saint's day and, especially, before Easter. The Prayer Book also provides a vigil for Pentecost.

Suggestions for Further Reading

Black, Vicki. *Welcome to the Book of Common Prayer.* Harrisburg, PA: Morehouse Publishing, 2005. This is a step-by-step introduction to the Book of Common Prayer, written for newcomers to the Episcopal Church.

Hatchett, Marion. *Commentary on the American Prayer Book.* New York: Seabury Press, 1980. This is the standard reference work for the 1979 Book of Common Prayer and the place where answers to most questions about it will be found.

Webber, Christopher L. *A New Metrical Psalter.* New York: Church Publishing, 1986. This book provides a useful alternative to plainsong and Anglican chant as a method of singing the psalms.

Other books that might be helpful for a deeper understanding of liturgical worship and the Anglican tradition include the following. Some of these books are out of print and most are not likely to be in your local library, but a good parish library should have them and a parish priest may be willing to loan them to those who care enough to ask.

On worship in general:

Dix, Dom Gregory. *The Shape of the Liturgy.* London: Dacre Press, 1945. A classic history of the development of the liturgy from its Jewish origins to the twentieth century; beautifully written, but also somewhat dated and more detailed than many people will want.

Otto, Rudolf. *The Idea of the Holy.* New York: Oxford University Press, 1950. This is one of the great books on the thoughts and feelings that underlie the human response to God.

Price, Charles, and Louis Weil. *Liturgy for Living.* New York: Seabury Press, 1979. Includes one chapter on the meaning of worship, one on the history of the Prayer Book, one on baptism, and then several chapters about the various sections of the Prayer Book; this was written for the ordinary church member and provides a good introduction.

Shepherd, Massey. *The Oxford American Prayer Book Commentary.* New York: Oxford University Press, 1950. This commentary is based on the 1928 Prayer Book and provides a facing page of commentary for every page of text for the whole book except the Psalter. While obviously out of date, it is still a helpful source of information and easy to use because of the format.

Underhill, Evelyn. *Worship.* New York: Harper and Brothers, 1936. A well-written history of the development of patterns of worship from primitive societies to the twentieth century, written by an English woman sixty years ago but still a good place to begin.

Webber, Christopher L. *Welcome to Sunday: An Introduction to Worship in the Episcopal Church.* Harrisburg, PA: Morehouse Publishing, 2002. A step-by-step guide to the Eucharist, the principal Sunday service of the Episcopal Church.

Index